CRAZY CREATURES OF THE ANIMAL KINGDOM

WHAT DO YOU KNOW ABOUT

UNDERGROUND ANIMALS?

FRANCINE TOPACIO

PowerKiDS
press

New York

Published in 2021 by The Rosen Publishing Group, Inc.
29 East 21st Street, New York, NY 10010

Portions of this work were originally authored by Marie Racanelli and published as *Underground Animals*. All new material in this edition authored by Francine Topacio.

Editor: Kara Murray
Book Design: Tanya Dellaccio

Cataloging-in-Publication Data

Names: Topacio, Francine.
Title: What do you know about underground animals?/ Francine Topacio.
Description: New York : PowerKids Press, 2021. | Series: Crazy creatures of the animal kingdom | Includes glossary and index.
Identifiers: ISBN 9781725319844 (pbk.) | ISBN 9781725319868 (library bound) | ISBN 9781725319851 (6pack)
Subjects: LCSH: Burrowing animals–Juvenile literature. | Underground ecology–Juvenile literature.
Classification: LCC QL756.15 T67 2021 | DDC 591.56'48–dc23

Manufactured in the United States of America

CPSIA Compliance Information: Batch #CSPK20. For Further Information contact Rosen Publishing, New York, New York at 1-800-237-9932.

Find us on

CONTENTS

ANIMALS IN HIDING.....................4

COZY UNDERGROUND HOMES..........6

DIFFERENT KINDS OF HOMES...........8

FINDING FOOD UNDERGROUND 10

ALL ABOUT
        UNDERGROUND ANIMALS...........12

TIME UNDERGROUND.....................14

BURROWS.................................16

UNDER THE SEAFLOOR 18

THE CICADA...............................20

HELPERS UNDERGROUND 22

GLOSSARY 23

INDEX.....................................24

WEBSITES 24

ANIMALS IN HIDING

The natural world is all around us. Outside your door, you might see a butterfly or a bird fly past or a squirrel climb up a tree. What about the animals and **insects** that you don't see or hear, though? Where are they?

Some of them are likely under the ground. Many living things make their homes underground. Some live under trees or large rocks. Some build underground **tunnels** and **burrows**, where they live and raise their young. If you dig in the soil or look under a rock, who knows what you might find? Let's dig into the hidden world of underground animals!

This chipmunk takes a look around outside its burrow. Some chipmunk burrows are like underground houses, with different rooms for sleeping, storing food, and even pooping!

COZY UNDERGROUND HOMES

All animals need food, water, and a place to live. Animals in underground homes are sheltered from the weather and many **predators**. Most predators are too large to fit inside a small animal's burrow.

A burrow or tunnel keeps animals out of the hot sun, which is very important for some animals. Earthworms, for example, breathe through their skin. The sun can dry out their skin and kill them. To stay safe, earthworms must spend most of their time under the ground.

Animals have a temperature at which their bodies work best. Underground homes keep animals warm when it gets too cool or cool when it gets too warm.

HOW STRANGE!

Prairie dog towns are made up of about 12 prairie dogs living together. The burrows have rooms for sleeping, caring for young, pooping, and listening for predators that might be outside.

Prairie dogs dig connected tunnels called prairie dog towns. They live in large communities and spend a lot of time working on their underground towns!

DIFFERENT KINDS OF HOMES

Animals live in different kinds of underground homes. A prairie dog lives in a burrow. Snakes live in holes, caves, or under rocks. Rabbits live in **warrens**. Hardworking ants live in **anthills** that have lots of tunnels under the ground.

Even some birds live underground! Have you ever heard of a burrowing owl? This kind of owl makes its home underground. It almost always lives in a burrow that another animal has left behind, although sometimes it digs its own. The owl lays its eggs, raises young, sleeps, and stores food in the burrow.

HOW STRANGE!

Burrowing owls don't usually dig their own burrows. They take over those dug by squirrels, prairie dogs, armadillos, tortoises, and skunks.

This burrowing owl stands outside its burrow. Unlike most owls, which hunt only at night, burrowing owls hunt during the day and at night.

FINDING FOOD UNDERGROUND

Many animals find the food they like to eat, such as soil, plant **roots**, or insects, underground and that's why they live there. Some of these animals may also become food for other animals that share their underground home.

Earthworms live underground because they eat soil. Moles live underground too. Guess what kind of food moles like to eat? If you guessed earthworms, then you're right. Moles mainly eat worms. In fact, they eat almost their body weight in worms every day! They also eat other underground animals and insects.

This mole is eating one of the many earthworms it will likely eat that day! Moles are always digging, which means they must eat a lot.

HOW STRANGE!

Moles are often blamed for eating plants in gardens, but they actually eat very little plant matter. However, their tunnels often damage plants so gardeners try to keep them out!

ALL ABOUT UNDERGROUND ANIMALS

1 **Cicadas** eat juice from tree roots.

2 Earthworms don't move through the dirt without a real home. They have tunnels where they sleep during the cold winter months.

3 The inside of an anthill needs to be deep enough underground to reach wet dirt. Otherwise, the ants' bodies will dry out.

4 Chipmunks hide their burrows from predators by placing leaves and sticks over the entrance hole. They make another entrance hidden by walls, trees, or rocks.

5 A prairie dog isn't a dog at all. It belongs to the rodent family.

6 Wombats save energy by staying cool inside their burrows during the heat of the day.

7 Troglobites are animals, such as eyeless spiders and millipedes, that live their whole lives in the darkest parts of caves. They can't see but can feel tiny **vibrations**.

8 All clams bury themselves in the sand. They use their muscular foot to burrow into the sand to stay away from predators.

9 Armadillos, such as the one shown here, live in underground dens and dig in the earth for insects to eat. Armadillos are covered in bony plates.

ARMADILLO

13

TIME UNDERGROUND

Do underground animals ever come out of their homes? Some animals do, while others spend most of their lives underground.

Moles and earthworms almost never come to the surface, or above the ground. The desert tortoise spends 95 percent of its life in burrows. If a desert tortoise lives around 80 years, it will spend about 76 years of its life inside its home! Desert tortoise burrows can be just a bit bigger than the tortoise's shell or sometimes larger. They have dozens of burrows spread out around their range, or the space in which they live and look for food. They move around and often share burrows.

HOW STRANGE!

Desert tortoises have different burrows for different seasons! In the spring and summer, they use short, shallow burrows that are close to the surface. Winter burrows are long and very deep underground.

Desert tortoises hibernate for the winter and rest during the summer. They are most active from March to June and from September to October.

BURROWS

There are some animals, such as chipmunks, that dig burrows for shelter, but they leave their burrows often to find food. Chipmunks make two types of burrows. One type has only one room. These are used for resting during the day. The other type has rooms to store food, a room to sleep in, and a room to give birth to babies. They spend the winter in these burrows.

Aardvarks are burrowers too. They rest in their burrows during the day and head out to look for food at night. Aardvarks are **nocturnal** animals. They are mainly active at night, but some aardvarks come out for a bit during the day to sun themselves!

HOW STRANGE!

When an aardvark finds a termite mound, it digs with its claws and uses its long, sticky tongue to get as many termites as it can.

Aardvarks live in Africa. They stay cool in their burrows during the day but when the sun sets, they use their powerful claws to dig up termites.

UNDER THE SEAFLOOR

The sea is home to underground animals too. A sand dollar is a sea animal that's shaped like a large coin and feels like hard, pressed sand. This animal buries itself on the sandy seafloor to hide from predators.

A sea cucumber will burrow into the ocean floor too. As it does this, it eats whatever bits of food it can find in the sand or mud. A sea cucumber doesn't stay in its burrow all the time. It will go back inside, though, if danger is approaching. Some eels are known to burrow in the sand as well.

Sand dollars bury themselves in the sand to stay safe when waters are rough and to eat. They stand on end, sticking up, when waters are calm.

19

THE CICADA

The cicada is **unique**. It has the longest underground life cycle of any insect. Some kinds live underground for up to 17 years!

A female cicada generally lays her eggs on a small branch. When the eggs break open, the newborn cicadas, or nymphs, fall to the ground and dig burrows for themselves. The nymphs stay in these burrows for anywhere from 2 to 5 years or 13 to 17 years, depending on what kind of cicada they are. During this time, the nymphs feed on tree roots. When they're ready, they dig to the surface and come out. They then shed their skin, **mate**, and lay eggs, dying soon after.

This cicada has just shed its skin and will fly up into the trees to find a mate. Females lay their eggs on tree branches.

HELPERS UNDERGROUND

Burrowing animals, such as moles and prairie dogs, sometimes have a bad reputation and are thought of as pests. On farms, horses can fall into burrow openings and hurt their legs. Running into mounds of dirt or burrows can damage farm machinery too. The truth is, though, that some of these underground animals have positive effects. Soil is made better by the digging of animals and also by their droppings. Some underground animals eat insects that might otherwise hurt crops.

Next time you're outside, look closely at the ground underneath you. Do you see signs of underground homes? The world of underground animals is beneath your feet!

GLOSSARY

aardvark: A burrowing African animal.

anthill: A mound made by ants as they remove sand from underground tunnels.

burrow: A hole an animal digs in the ground for shelter.

cicada: A large insect that makes a loud buzzing sound.

insect: A small animal that often has six legs and wings.

mate: To come together to make babies.

nocturnal: Active mainly during the night.

predator: An animal that kills other animals for food.

root: The part of a plant or tree that is underground.

tunnel: A passage under or through something, such as the ground.

unique: Special or different from anything else.

vibration: A small, quick movement.

warren: A rabbit hole.

INDEX

A
AARDVARK, 16, 17
AFRICA, 17
ANT, 8, 12
ARMADILLO, 8, 13

B
BURROWING OWL, 8, 9

C
CHIPMUNK, 5, 12, 16
CICADA, 12, 20, 21
CLAM, 13

E
EARTHWORM, 6, 10, 11, 12, 14
EEL, 18

I
INSECT, 10, 20, 22

M
MILLIPEDE, 13
MOLE, 10, 11, 14, 22

P
PRAIRIE DOG, 6, 7, 8, 12, 22

R
RABBIT, 8

S
SAND DOLLAR, 18, 19
SEA CUCUMBER, 18
SKUNK, 8
SNAKE, 8
SPIDER, 13
SQUIRREL, 8

T
TERMITE, 16, 17
TORTOISE, 8, 14, 15
TROGLOBITE, 13

W
WOMBAT, 12

WEBSITES

Due to the changing nature of Internet links, PowerKids Press has developed an online list of websites related to the subject of this book. This site is updated regularly. Please use this link to access the list: www.powerkidslinks.com/ccotak/underground